Autumn and
the Bad Bean

Autumn and the Bad Bean

A child's life with cancer

Written and Illustrated by
Gordon Hoeft Jr.

POOKANELLI PRESS
Bristow, VA

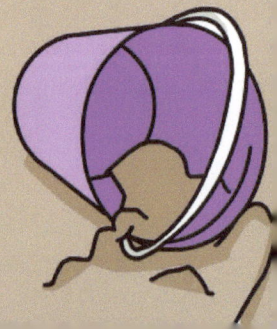

This book is dedicated to my precious daughter
Autumn Nicole Hoeft. You lived, loved, and laughed
better than anyone I have ever known.
We love and miss you dearly.

foreword

This book is about one brave girl's battle with cancer. It is my hope that her story will comfort, inspire, and give hope to those children who live with similar conditions or another life-threatening illness. It is my further intention to raise awareness of childhood cancer in all its forms, and highlight how underfunded both by public and private organizations childhood cancer research is.

Please refer to the sections in the back of the full version of this book, also available, for important information about present cancer research. This includes statistics about childhood cancer funding, charitable organizations, who to contact for funding reform and a glossary of some commonly used terms.

I hope readers come away from this book with the intention to make a difference in the fight against childhood cancer from making donations to research and charitable organizations or by contacting your state senator and representatives on the issue of childhood cancer funding reform. Patients and parents are in overwhelming need of support in areas of quality-of-life assistance to treatment-funding for the hopeful survival of the children and an eventual cure.

These children though sick, are still children and deserve every chance at life. They are our future as any healthy child, and potentially the difference-makers in a better tomorrow.

G.H.
Bristow, VA
May, 2014

Autumn and the Bad Bean

Autumn Nicole is an energetic little girl, who lives in a very happy home. She has flowing golden brown hair that spirals into ringlets and a smile that lights up a room.

Autumn is also a very cheerful girl and loves her family very much. She loves her pet cat, Rusty and dog Kenobi, too.

She loves being pretty and enjoys
dressing up as most little girls do.
Her favorite costume is her fairy princess outfit.

She dresses up and makes pretend food for her many
adoring stuffed animals in her playtime kitchen.
She loves to make believe and dream.

Autumn is also very brave and adventuresome.
She rides her toy 4-wheeler after her father as he jogs.
She loves going fast!

At night, Autumn curls up with her mommy and they read story books together before going to bed.

One night, Autumn woke her parents because her head hurt. She didn't feel very well. Her parents gave her medicine and it seemed to help her head. She woke the next morning feeling better and had a wonderful day.

However, night-after-night the headache kept returning. Her mommy, knowing Autumn was too young for such headaches, decided to make a doctor's appointment.

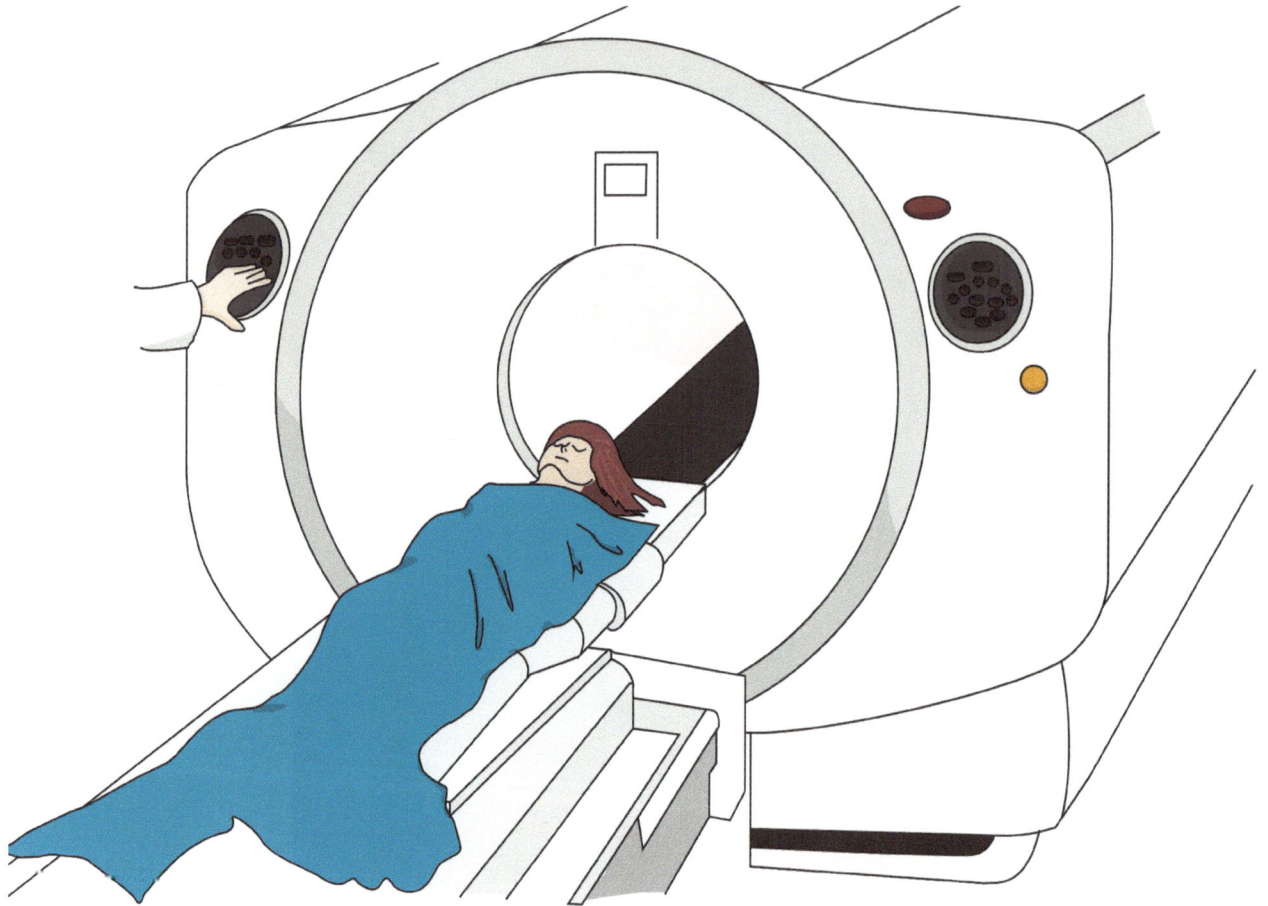

The next day at the hospital, the doctors were
confused and couldn't find anything wrong with
Autumn. Autumn's mommy, fearing something
serious was wrong, asked for an X-ray, which the
doctors had made. The picture showed the Bad Bean.

Everyone was sad. The Bad Bean was in little
Autumn's head giving her bad headaches. The
doctors seemed optimistic and said they could make
her feel better. No one knew then that the bean in
Autumn's head was the meanest Bad Bean of them all.

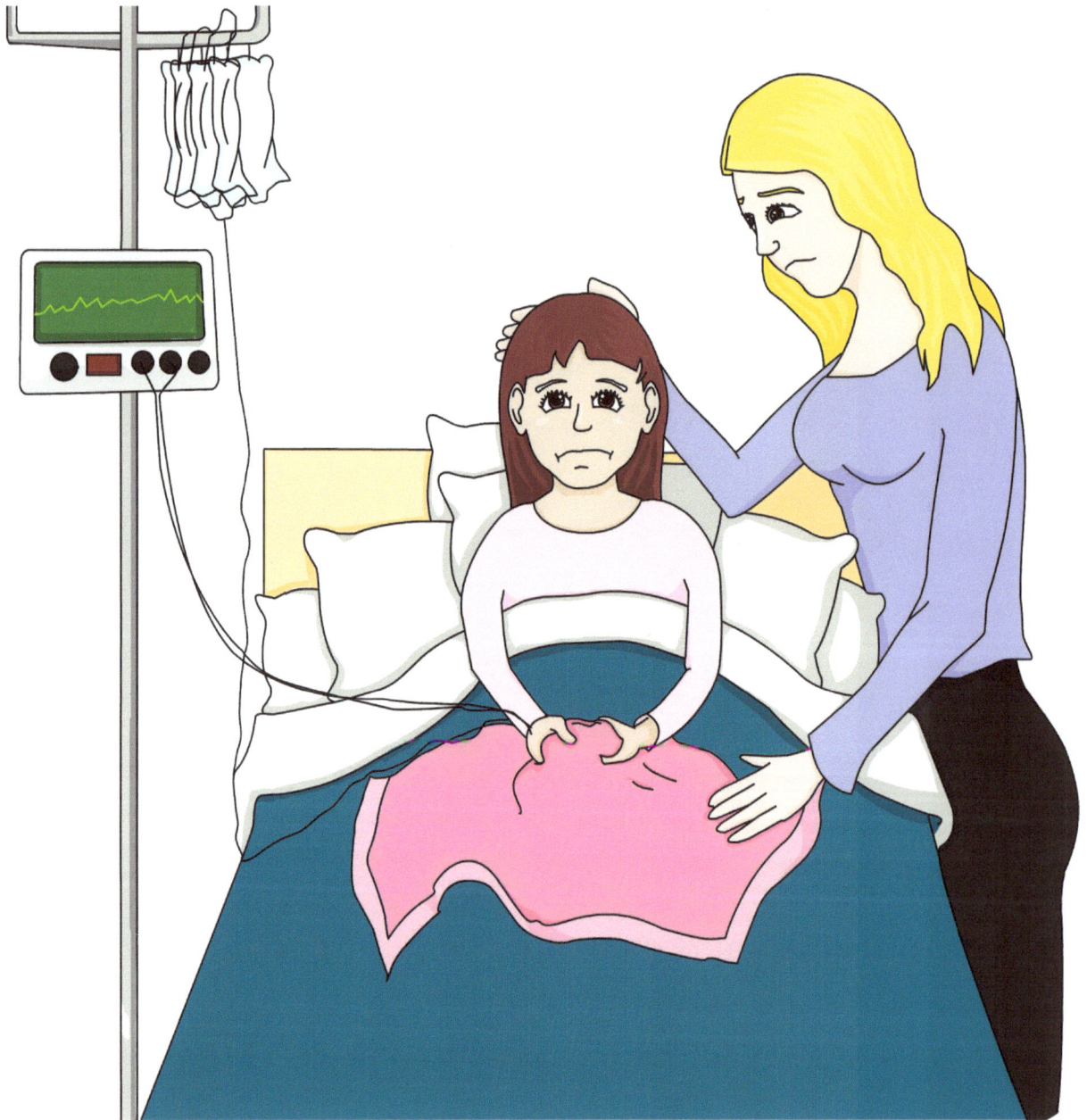

The following morning, Autumn was made
ready for surgery so the doctors could look
at the Bad Bean and see if they could take it
out of her head. They told her and her parents
that they were going to have to shave a spot
on Autumn's head so they can look inside.

Autumn bravely agreed and went into
the surgery room. After the doctors finished
and Autumn woke up in the recovery room,
Autumn had a small bald spot on her head and
some stitches. Her mommy, waiting to hold her tight,
gave her a new stuffed animal for being so brave.

One day passed and the doctor had bad news.
They couldn't get the Bad Bean to leave.
It was very stubborn. Autumn didn't understand
why the Bad Bean was with her, but trusted the
doctors and her parents to do what was right.
She was determined to fight.

The doctors quickly put a plan together.
They said the only way to fight such
a Bad Bean was to attack it with
special medicine and radiation. Unfortunately,
Autumn would have to make a lot of doctor visits.

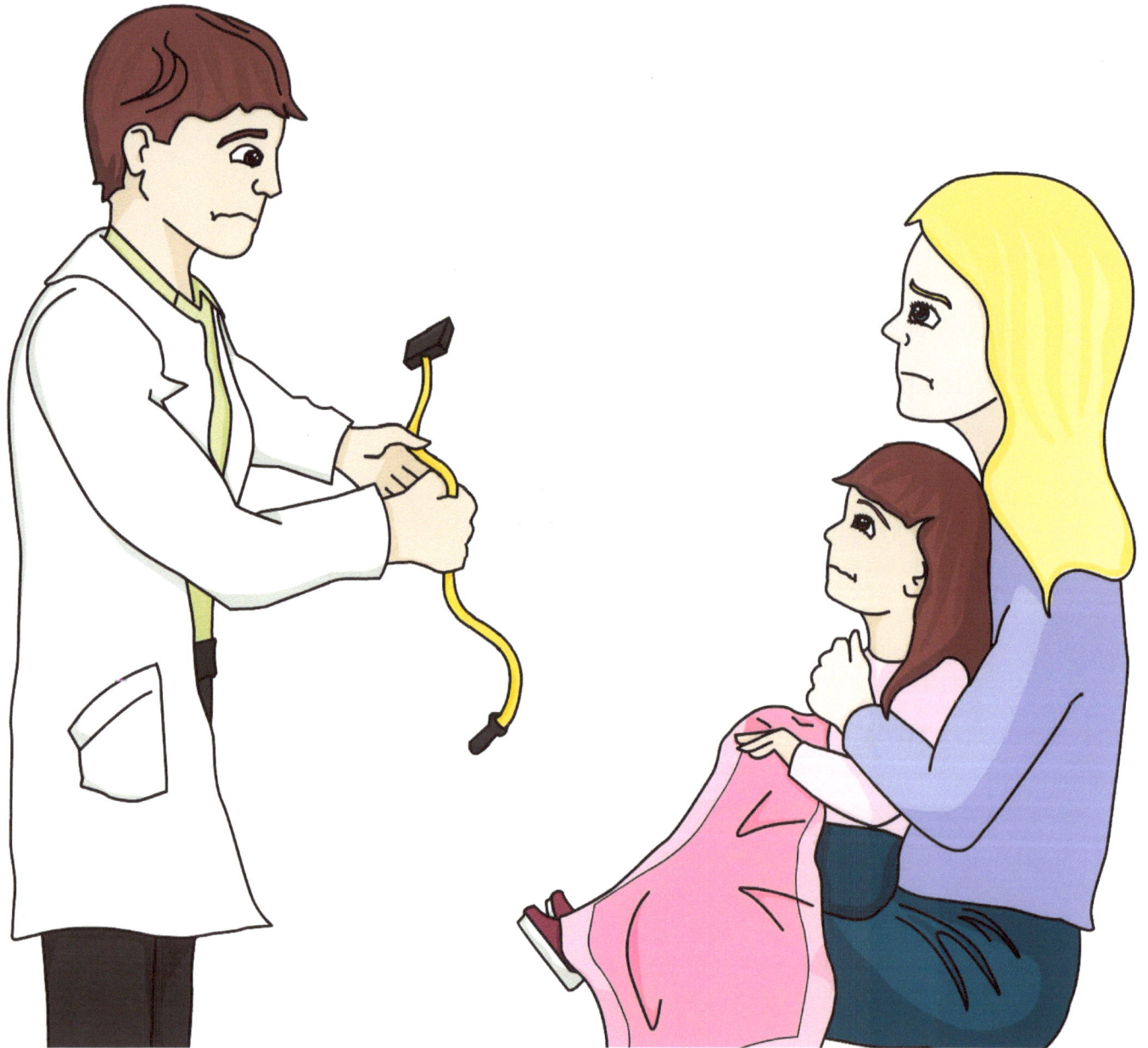

Treatment began right away. Autumn was introduced to Tubey. Tubey was a long lanky yellow tube that would deliver medicine directly into her bloodstream. Tubey would help fight the Bad Bean. Autumn wasn't too sure about Tubey, but the next day she went into surgery again so he could be put in place to help. Once again, Autumn woke to find another stuffed animal friend waiting for her as well as her new friend Tubey.

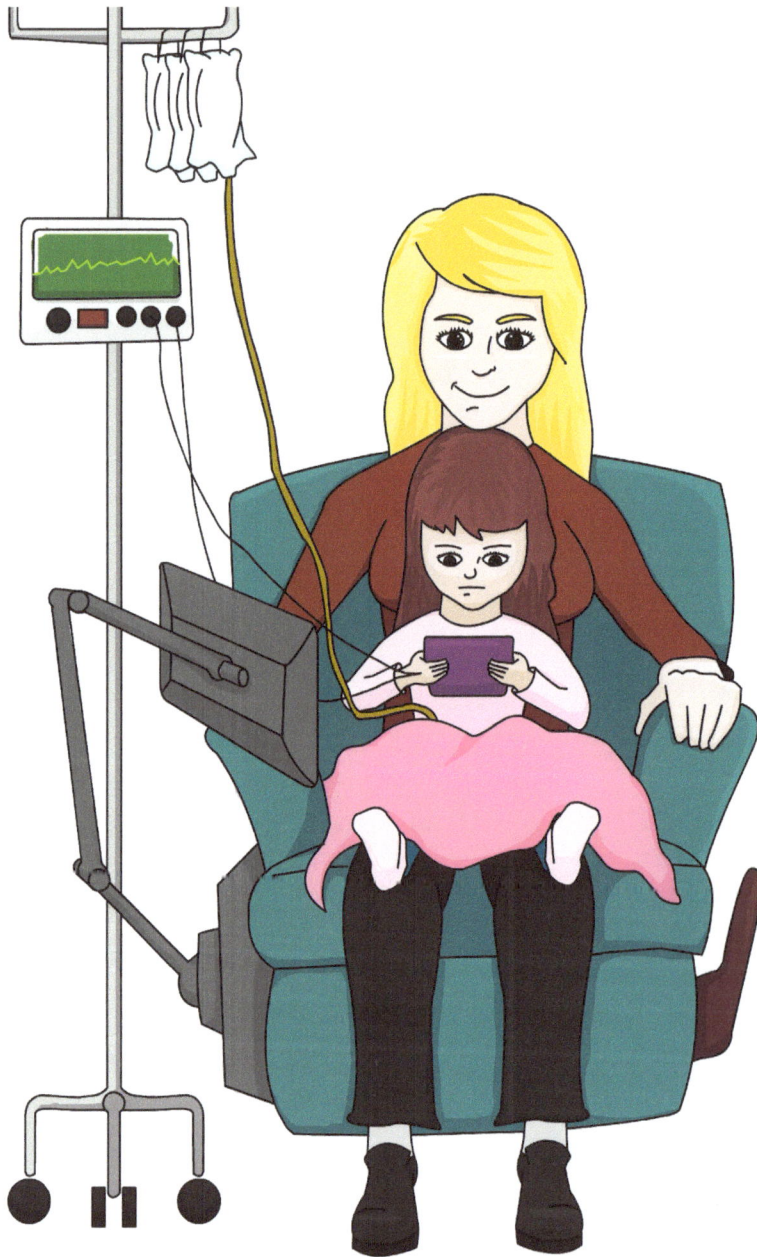

Therapy started soon after. She was introduced to her new doctor in the pink coat and the staff at the special hospital and shown all of the cool activities they had there to help fill the time.

Autumn's favorite was arts and crafts, but she loved watching movies and playing her video games too.

Autumn began to lose her hair and soon she
had none left on her head. She tried to wear
a wig but she decided it was too scratchy. Instead,
Autumn accepted her baldness. Sometimes she would
wear cute headbands with flowers on them for fun.

The medicine made Autumn very sick.
Sometimes she would be tired or not at all hungry but
mostly both. She would often have to take long rests.
However, she could still be quite active riding her bike,
going to the playground and playing with her friends.

Weeks went by and Autumn had triumphant
dreams about fighting the Bad Bean alongside
Tubey. She and Tubey would blast the Bad Bean
with their super powers, and each time he would
get smaller and less scarey. She was very sure
she could beat the mean ol' Bad Bean.

Examinations of her spine were done regularly, to make sure the Bad Bean hadn't brought any friends and spread them to other parts of her body and, luckily he hadn't. They caught him before he could call his friends. Autumn didn't like the examinations very much even though she never remembered them when they were over.

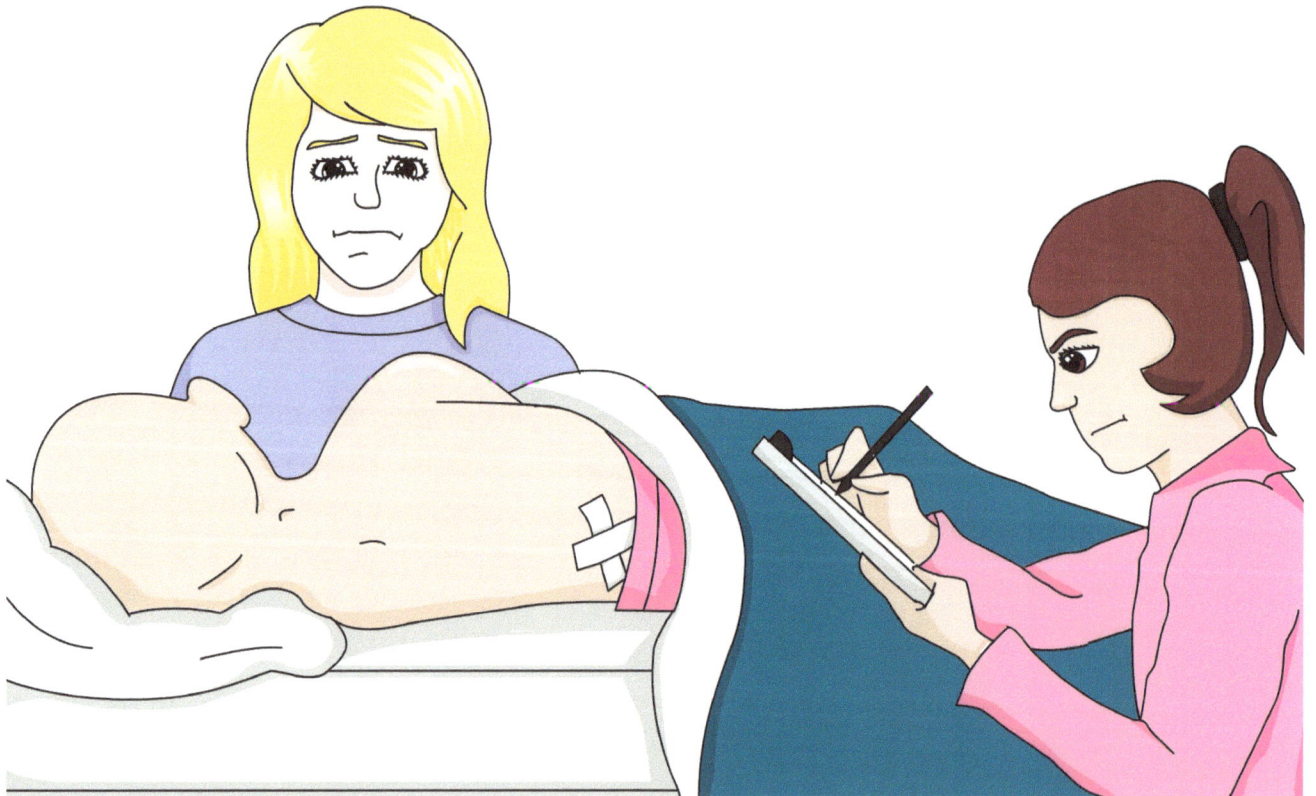

The doctor in the pink coat came in one day and said that they no longer could see the Bad Bean! She thought the Bad Bean was either gone or so small the radiation would take him out when treatment started.

Autumn was to go to Houston, Texas for specially targeted radiation treatments. Autumn had never been on a plane before and was excited about the trip. Her daddy got wheels for her car seat and pushed her all the way to the plane.

Once there, Autumn met her new doctor,
Dr. Wolfe, and she thought he was very funny.
She also met her new radiation therapy doctor,
Dr. Hans, who was friendly also.

Autumn loved Texas. Her new home away
from home had the best pool ever! On days
when she was feeling well she could swim all day!

Sadly, radiation also made Autumn tired and
left her skin sun burned. She didn't like that
part very much because she couldn't go to the pool.

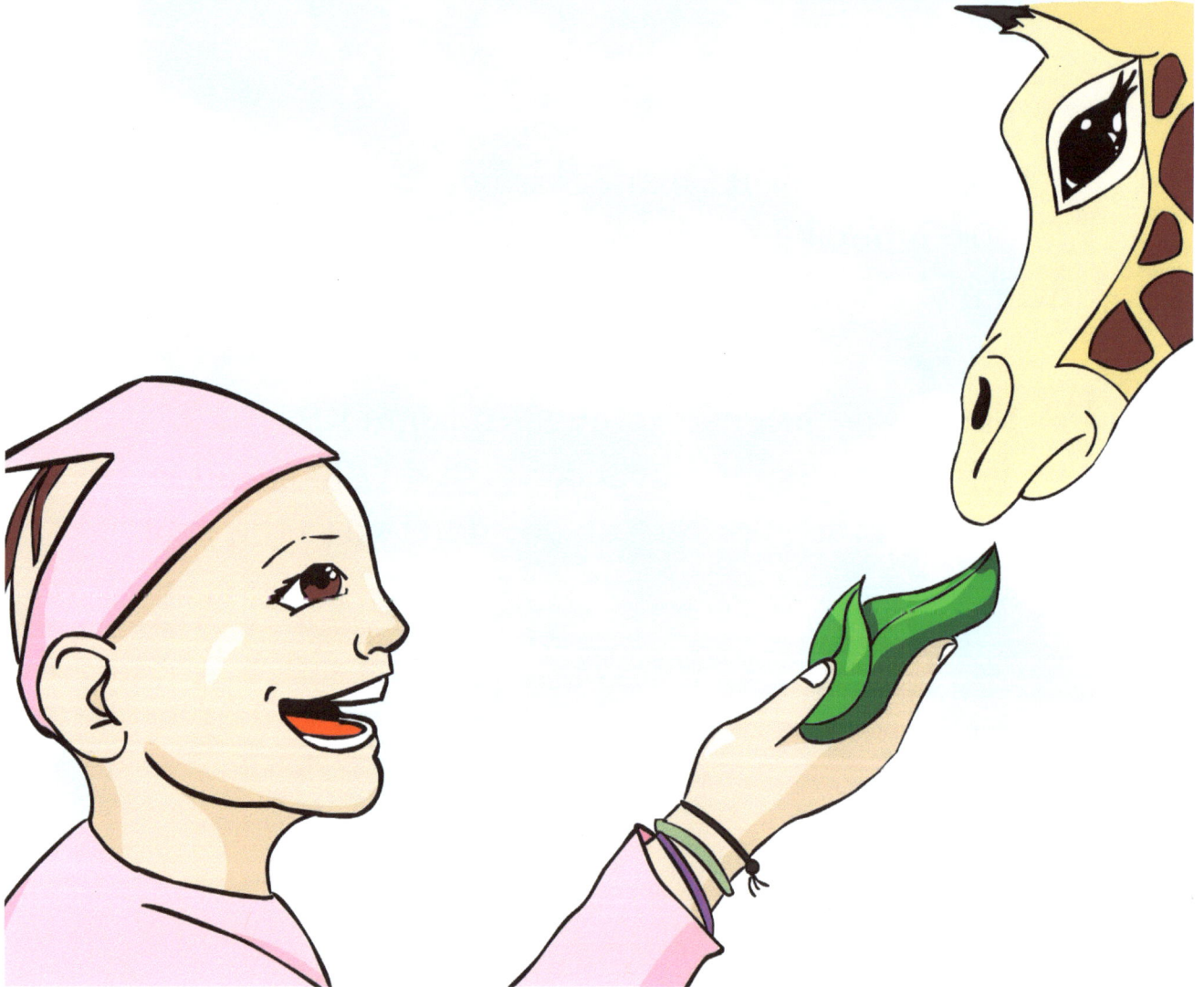

Her parents kept her spirits up as best they
could, and took her to Kemah, a nearby
town, where there was an amusement park!

Autumn rode some of the rides, but had the
most fun dancing to a live band and playing
on the playground with other kids.

On her good days,
Autumn did so many fun things!
She got to visit the Children's Museum,
the Aquarium and the Houston Zoo!

On one wonderful day, Autumn was
taught to ice skate at the Galleria Mall and
best of all, bounce so high on the extreme
flyer trampoline—her absolute favorite!

Autumn had many wonderful days.
She finished her medicine and radiation therapy.
Dr. Wolfe and Dr. Hans agreed the Bad Bean was gone.
Autumn didn't dream about him anymore.

Autumn said "Good-bye" to Dr. Wolfe,
Dr. Hans and even Tubey. Tubey was no
longer needed and stayed behind in Texas.
Autumn was sad but glad to not need him.

Autumn felt great in the weeks after all of the treatments ended. Her hair began to grow back, and she could do everything she used to.

She was back at full speed going to the pool, riding her bike, and enjoying the playground as she used to. She even went to the beach, which was a lot of fun.

That fall, she went on her Make-A-Wish Nickelodeon cruise and met all of her favorite characters. It was the best time she ever had and made up for all she had been through.

Autumn had many splendid days.
She began kindergarten the following
year, and loved every minute, especially
riding the big yellow bus all by herself.
She even met a boy who was a special friend.

This single volume was designed, written,
edited and illustrated by Gordon Hoeft.
A special thanks to Maureen Lauran for
proofing and guidance. The text is Century
Schoolbook with Curlz MT for display.
Printed on a digital press in the spring of 2014.
Designed and bound origianlly at
George Mason University, Fairfax,Virginia.

www.ingramcontent.com/pod-product-compliance
Lightning Source LLC
Chambersburg PA
CBHW061053090426
42740CB00003B/133